Published by the author in 2019. ISBN: 978-0-578-55227-9

© Zachary Horvitz

All rights reserved. May not be reproduced or distributed without permission. No work within may be published in its entirety without the written permission of the author. Partial quotations for reviews and references are permitted.

Cover design by Robin Herman

# Without Origin

~

Zachary Horvitz

| | | | |
|---|---|---|---|
| Olam | 1 | Kyle | 28 |
| Planets Turn | 2 | Station Grey | 29 |
| Queen of Swords | 3 | Young Alaina | 30 |
| Talmud | 4 | Evening | 31 |
| July | 5 | Zoe | 32 |
| Yaakov | 6 | Even Mount Sumeru | 33 |
| Lexicon | 7 | Beginning | 34 |
| Winter Cosmogony | 8 | Mercutio | 35 |
| Nachman's Chair | 9 | Merlin | 36 |
| The Headless... | 10 | Waves | 37 |
| Heretics | 11 | Reception | 38 |
| If the Owl... | 12 | Marlowe | 39 |
| Friend | 13 | Vilna Gaon | 40 |
| Polemos | 14 | Seder | 41 |
| No Taste | 15 | Beautiful Gardens | 42 |
| Summer | 16 | Yester Night | 43 |
| Banzai | 17 | Echad | 44 |
| Exodus | 18 | Compass | 45 |
| Waiting | 19 | Naropa | 46 |
| Breakfast | 20 | Minerva Again | 47 |
| Four Octobers | 21 | First Thing | 48 |
| Landscape Artist | 22 | Christmas | 49 |
| First Morning | 23 | Shekhinah | 50 |
| Jus Soli | 24 | Chen | 51 |
| Sidney | 26 | Bipolarity | 52 |
| Béla, Planting | 27 | | |

*An alphabetical table of contents appears on page 54.*

**Olam**

The gravestone marks that side you cannot reach
with any mind. Ivy overgrows the grey,
but there is no one beneath the slab.
Walking around, standing still, or saying kaddish,
your presence in the cemetery there
is another's every absence.
Thus you resurrect the dead.
Suddenly the world to come, for which another
waited, looks much like the world
in which some now wait. Sun illuminates
everything that blooms, including slabs of stone.
Recursive night falls once more.
What is called the Ancient of Days
is a single ancient day.

**Planets Turn**

You sleep beneath the nocturnal sheen.
Musical notes like tiny seizures,
an electric tickle when waking.
All beings lead a double life
until night and day merge
without mercy. Planets
turn without hurry, wherefore
do you run? How many psalms
until your task is complete?
What speaks, hypnotic,
as though it were I, and we?

**Queen of Swords**

At the heart of all seeming things,
the sadness of the queen of swords.
And one who quells without a weapon
relentless winter. The theatre of war
is not for thespians, nor is
the battlefield a stage. Upon what plane
can blackened ice begin
to form, can kingdoms mourn
the harm of morbid play?

**Talmud**

*Olam* is another word
for the elusive Godot.
What will never come
is also the one place
that never goes,
where Lurianic sparks
are everywhere scattered
and waiting is wonderful
when always there is task,
the tikkun of taking tea
or telling tales. Being together
is the ordinary telos
worth our transience —
for the Lord is not our friend
as the Talmud warns,
but you have been to me,
and I sometimes
imperfectly to you,
in this realm of
sometimes passing.

**July**

In the basement of a house in Nova Scotia
we sat together on a single dryer. Your dress
was long, the color of your eyes.
It was the emerald color of your eyes.
It was the color of Rimbaud's green nights.
And Lorca's green, the color
of his mind. That August, in the silence
of a different house, by another sea, I
played a game: if the crumpled
paper thrown across the room
falls in the wicker basket, this girl will
be my wife. For certain then.

**Yaakov**

Adrift in the dimension of dreams,
I saw you on a hospital tv screen,
performing morning prayers
across an ocean. Folklore tells of thirty-six
lamedvavnik, who keep this narrow bridge
of a breaking world intact.
We might be missing one or two,
but such dreams remind me
of the spaces, liminal or small,
for one called you.

**Lexicon**

Among the many words I didn't know
before I met you, I remember three:
*prolific, crass,* and *brine.* You called me prolific
because I was always writing poems
enumerating the crass things I would do
to you whose body smells like brine.
Five years, and my brain has made room
for new vocabularies, but my whole
self still yearns for you.

**Winter Cosmogony**

In the beginning God absconded.
Without origin, the human flower blooms.
Without destiny, no one is entombed.
He requires no creation, nor absence
of creation, though meaningful snow
falls everywhere at night, touching eyelids
and toes, seeping through strong socks
where we go. I have forgotten all about
the Rebbe's Tanya, but a niggun
climbs, note by note inside
these living wires.

**Nachman's Chair**

Like one seated in Reb Nachman's regal chair,
You are afloat upon the globe of earth.
A universal monarch of the whole affair,
Without thought of gain or loss, death or birth.
Open then the forehead's treasure trove,
A portal to prismatic colored worlds,
Where sound and light are made of lucid love,
And insubstantial thoughts like clouds unfurl.
Speak dead tongues to all those happy beings,
Who wake from slumber with your helpful chants,
Which make the seamless be just as it seems,
Among the anthropoids, trees and plants.
A huge procession round your primal seat,
All things at once abound about your feet.

### The Headless…

The headless horseman knows a secret
the Holocene won't reveal. Holding on
to body and mind, a corpse flounders
in the midst of muddy flowers.
Letting the head go: a flowering.
How many yellow vines escape,
how many snakes? The blue diamond
swallowed instead of Kali's blade
which takes the timid. Out of extinction,
a mind to mind transmission. Midnight,
and the diamond already lodged
inside so many skulls. Here is the hydra,
from your own hippocampus expunged.

## Heretics

At midnight the bathing room is a monastic cell.
There the crypto-Christian listens to Come Thou Fount
(Of Every Blessing.) Sometimes the smallest room in a
    house
is where the laughter and the music are
appropriate most. At the apotheosis
of Judaic thought, emerge characters like Christ
or Sabbatai Tzvi, who both raised the kiddush cup
after a final sabbath meal. Who took forbidden loves.
"This heaven shall pass, and the one that is coming
shall pass." They praised the passing, knew no maze
of time, nor eternal resting place. At midnight
there is one without particular faith, nor faithless,
bathing, composing songs, laughing
while other music plays. The orthodoxy
    excommunicated
Spinoza for seeing God in geometries of nature.
For staying in his attic too long, that miniature
    synagogue,
where all the magic was.

**If the Owl...**

If the Owl of Minerva flies at dusk, let it be our dusk.
If history means less and less, let us mean more
to each other. The sword I fought with was plastic,
though I was able to decapitate my foe.
That was what the dream time at least showed.
What I should say is, unmoored, the years
do not accumulate. It is not like reaching
the plateau of some formidable temple
longed for by Spanish explorers of a century
now fabled. It is not like that at all. Here
a new telos gathers, its wings begin to spread
and we are suddenly no longer talking
about Athena's owl, but a greater bird
at least in girth. The Garuda overhead. The clouds
perforated by a play of light. The dusk no less
a triumph than a failure of that light. And foe's head
dreamed, having the look of mine. Eye-whites
confused. Irises upward, the contorted gaze of time.

**Friend**

Friend, don't let too much dust obscure
the primordial mirror that's with you.
Such motes can't sully what's always there.
You reflected me, and I reflected you,
though our true faces have no eyes
and only light illuminates itself.
What happened long ago?
What can the future harm?
What looks through all beings is only
that mirrored light, all at once,
astres burning, prior to all gods,
those we make and those who visit
us in sleep or in poetic reverie.
Friend, let's forget the astres, gods, and light.
Let's forget the finger and the moon
and the one who's pointing now.
I love you, from before beginning
you've been just as you are,
you'll be what is, that's it.

**Polemos**

On the night of my 29th birthday,
I found myself alongside Mbappe
at the far end of sleep.
We were to take a nameless beach,
clothed in centuries-old
war garments, like prized horses
at the starting gate of the dream.
Unleashed, birth and death
was a single implosion,
out of the womb of space
into greater space. Our green berets
soaking up the brine. A soccer star
and a poet on the front lines,
restored to time, without second thought—
in the forever charge, cloudless above.

**No Taste**

Thunder and the sound of rain
hitting the skylight.
Jasmine tea, over-brewed.
In my mouth, no taste
of bitterness at all.
The sweetness of never
having kissed you.

**Summer**

In the warm Holocene of summer
you made of the microcosm a messianic age.
A Starbucks cup deteriorating in the sun,
cold coffee spilled on marble stone.
Pillowed by light more powerful than Isaac Luria's
Eyn Sof. A perfect blindness in that illumination.
Lucid and mindless. There are notes composed
by many rebbes that sometimes reach composure
in spite of chaos. A simple niggun
like the hum of your voice as bodies
and buildings prematurely tremble
seeking the end of days. The world a narrow
bridge, but a bridge all the same.

**Banzai**

Is it romantic to say that soldiers have what poets lack?
Georges Bataille (curious... French for battle)
yearned for the negative wagering
of his own life. I don't know if he failed.
Certainly the poem is an implicit failure...
(aimed at declaring absence.)
A flower does not preach, said U.G.
He might have been wrong.
I love the look of words surrounded by so much space,
perhaps as much as what's declared.
A soldier's banzai charge is like a star
that smolders across a peaceful void
infinitely larger than all bodies and minds.
So die like a single flower drowning in winter rain
or like tumbleweed blown about by wind
or like a fantastic fountain spilling dark matter
from multiple heads. I really don't know
what's better. Could you say?

**Exodus**

Before the techno-gnosticism of the elite,
the earth was already beyond itself.
A paradise shooting through ethereal space.
"This heaven shall pass, and the one
that is coming shall pass," said
the paragon of Eden. Today
some billionaires are plotting escape
into worlds more virgin. I'd rather burn
with it all, offering everything
to the life-giving fire, in sublime flames
of war, or in the final solar storm.

**Waiting**

Though I have flown two dozen times,
I still get scared.
I used to say the Sh'ma before every flight.
It is comparable to Ave Maria but not really.
I cannot sleep tonight. I am thinking about how soon
you will be in the sky, on the way to see me
and others who will also be happy to see you.
I have recited ancient Hebrew
for the sake of many, but never prior
to anyone else's flight. Soon you will be in the sky.
The Jewish Ave Maria is a spontaneous
utterance you inspire.

**Breakfast**

We almost died that day. I remember the car swerve,
your father's Polish curse. I remember how good
the bagels were at breakfast. I remember how crisp
the water. And the laughter of your father, over tea.
I remember his baldness and his beard.
The tall ceiling and the dark table.
I remember your father's lover, how ugly
and how loving, as she ate. I remember
the conversation, about eating. "One should eat
slowly. One should chew one's food slowly,
as do monks." I remember most the smell of bergamot
on your skin, as if you had taken a bath
infused with sachets of Earl Grey. Surely all breakfasts
have been failures since that day.

**Four Octobers**

 Although there was culinary lavender in a plastic bowl
on my night table, my nose fell
instead into the tight crease of a black book.
Although you were waiting for me across the distance
of exactly four Octobers, you had fallen
each separate season on all fours, and not for me.
Although there was a purple vase for the unspecified
if not plastic house plants you gave me, I put them in a bottle
of coke. I put them on my night table, in a bottle of coke.
Four Octobers ago you promised the tight crease of your
lavender cunt. When it is cold, I take the flower buds
from the plastic bowl, and brew them in a tea.

## Landscape Artist

You call yourself a landscape artist
but in fact you cultivate cannabis
on the roof of your shoddy apartment
on which it is raining more often than not.
There was a time when you called me
wordsmith, silver-tongued. The people
in the world whom you envy mostly grew up
in rural Pennsylvania, not the Amish
but something close. How have you come
to envy yourself? Over the phone
you used the phrase, "When we
were growing up." Did you wear braces
when you were growing up, the dentist asks.
I suspect that your classmate hung himself
because he was afraid of one day dying.
Does the cannabis keep you going
when the green landscape is flooded
with grey, more often than not?

**First Morning**

On the first morning of the world,
God gave himself a gift —
an anonymous gift, called wakefulness.
He didn't ask for anything.
He didn't ask for it. Like all gifts
it was terrible. Imagine
the burden of stars.
Imagine the burden of mountains,
the burden of hearts.
Imagine a birthday
on which none of your friends
or distant relatives or parents
were present, a birthday on which
everyone else was present,
including the dead (or only the dead!) —
imagine now the burden
of other times you carry.
They left early, too soon —
so soon. How could you
make out a particular face
from this general sea of faces?
How could you write one thank-you note?
 At night the shame would be vast.

**Jus Soli**

Since 1998 I have been ready
to claim citizenship. Chirac, I have been ready.
For sporting goods I shop almost exclusively
at Decathlon — in dreams, I walk
beneath the Arc de Triomphe
to Decathlon, where I am with my father
buying the right cleats
for artificial turf. Chirac, I cannot blame you
enough. Chirac, I love the hard assonance of
your name too much, to go on making blame.
Chirac, it has been since '98. So much
has happened, we moved soon after
Lady Diana died. Chirac, you would not
believe how old my father is
these days. You would not believe
how deaf our dog from Normandy,
how almost blind she is. I am not even writing this
in 2008. It is three years since
the end of our football team's
golden generation. Chirac, you too wore
the number 10, and fell in love
with the balding Algerian

and thanked him when he failed us in '06.
Chirac I am not talking about sports.
I am haunting you with synecdoches
for my urban ghost. Jacques Chirac, I love you
more than your immigration policies,
and those Nicolas Sarkozy maintains.
I find them untenable today.

## Sidney

Grandfather, I was made from you.
I inherited your limited palate.
I inherited your personally annotated
copies of Karl Popper and Frost.
(Your margin notes
are a higher order of thought.
I cherish the intimations of your penmanship
more than this literary inheritance.)
I have your digestive
issues, but I am not a drinker —
I don't intend to pass as many stones.
I once had a vocation
for law school, but where did that go?
In college you were on a football team
and so am I, in spite of definitions.
You owned a hat business.
That has nothing to do with
anything but I think that is
cool. On airplanes I have looked for you
among clouds. In my seventh year
I asked the pilot
to fly through the thickest cumulus
that I might find you there.

**Béla, Planting**

Béla is planting mushrooms. He stole them
from the kitchen. "It is a political move."
I do not doubt him. At dusk he passes
in silence beyond the fields. His bicycle
is blue, his sweater's color obscured.

## Kyle

I

The word Seder in Hebrew means order.
Minute attention to Talmudic law
is a piety akin to the way Romans
waged war, or Barcelona plays football.

II

On Yom Kippur, Kyle Keymaram never
plays football. On Yom Kippur we lost our game.

III

The tedium of secular life is the failure to
suspend disbelief. The Shabbos is holy
because bread and candles are holy,
because it is holy to gather
in the silence before sundown,
in the silence of candles and bread.

**Station Grey**

It's almost bedtime.
I'm not so tired.
I want to listen
to the saddest song
any voice has ever sung.
Do you have a request?
There's one I love.
The title: Station Grey.
Those two words are great.
I think of trains.
I think of the color of rain.
I think of you —
Oh, Station Grey

**Young Alaina Dancing**

You are the Snowqueen poised
before a twirl. Snowflakes
yield to your crown, yield to you.
The snowplough does not threaten
to parse your kingdom into heaps.
Your poise is winter's eternity
which does not vanish but is
hidden in spring. Why did you
ever stop dancing?

**Evening**

It is sometimes unbearable,
to be saturated with lush sound,
salutations in the dark, music
that comes like arms
waving in perpetual goodbye —
It is sometimes unbearable:
a pair of emerald eyes
that mortifies the senses. It is
unbearable, to breathe familiar
pheromones, to become only a nose.

## Zoe

I set out to terraform the earth & ingest the sunlight.
 I stained my skin with chlorophyll & urinated
 in the unkempt grass. I grew nostalgic for
  Scandinavian
climates, shimmering tundra, ice like frozen glass
reflecting sunbeams. There is no end to my wanderlust
for ascetic atmospheres. Of the five elements, ether is
  my queen,
who supervises whole stars and the star that feeds me.
What began as somatic cleansing ended in romance
with celestial fire: red giants, blue dwarfs.

**Even Mount Sumeru**

Even Mount Sumeru can crumble.
The library at Alexandria once burned, as you well
    know.
But who can blow away the dust to somewhere exiled
when exile also is a house of dust? Who can put out the
    flames
when smoke reaches always to the spheres?
Perhaps in another world there is one singing
just like me. When a globe of words is no more
again exhausted stars make room
for other realms and times, where winged creatures
of winter might evolve, mouths full
of melody, eyes full of anarchy.

**Beginning**

The teenager thinks Zen has
something to do with black robes
and fancy pillows. In Nova Scotia,
falls in love with Acadian shores
and a girl with wisdom eyes painted
on her back. Goes on believing the
real work is yet to be, somewhere
within monastic halls, where serious
ascetics keep their sacred bond.
Everything already illuminated by a
perfect sun, still he seeks the living
fire. That black dragon jewel,
everywhere all the while.

## Mercutio

Once before Queen Mab had been with him.
The sovereign faerie's heart was sometime tied
To that young soldier's all too garrulous mind.
Only the glow of amethyst in her eyes,
That gentle violet light, could keep him quiet.
What did Romeo know of such a spell?
How many ballroom kisses could compare?
All sprites return to air, at last abscond
Their crystal gaze, combusting many fates.
Mercutio didn't need the king of cats,
Good Tybalt, to entice a public duel.
And Romeo didn't need to come between.
The consequence was hanging in the stars
When Mab departed from Mercutio's dreams.

**Merlin**

When the  speech of elders wears out, who can
   guide you?
Merlin has left the forest and there are only trees.
The charismatic words of the wise ones sink
into elemental earth. The body is stiff with grief
but the mind is gladdened. How ancient am I
who have found no wisdom at all.

**Waves**

Waves are the ocean blooming
into a way station of sound.
Roses ask
for life inside our speech.
Names are often cast
like nets about all things.
Sleep is the womb of all things,
& dreams are the only things born.
Asleep, you named me before
I was borne into the family of things.

**Reception**

Kabbalah is not an abstruse subject,
despite the obscure project
of many scholars and their fun.
Do you remember Rashi's saying
in our favorite movie? (Receive
with simplicity everything that happens
to you.) Kabbalah means reception,
as in a perfect touchdown pass...
Our life is a constant flying away, a floating
in the hands of Hashem. The chair you sit on
sits on nothing. The bed you lay in has
no ground. Let yourself be held
in the only moment there is, the moment of is,
a Kabbalat Shalom.

**Marlowe**

Kit Marlowe died at age mere twenty nine,
For epicurism and other erstwhile crimes,
Irreligious jaunts or jovial religion;
One marvels at his didactic precision.
Two years hence I will outlive his lifespan
And thank some stars for keeping me intact
To tell of lesser feats, though happy plans
To be merry, and to pen poetic tracts.

**Vilna Gaon**

It must be lonely to be the Vilna Gaon
Enclosed in a room with nothing but books
No wine to share with guests
It must be lonely to always go beyond
The astounding trap of mortal earth

**Seder**

It's best to stay composed before the thing itself.
What is the thing itself? Not a thing at all.
The Alter Rebbe, Zalman of Liadi, knew this
in his time, despite the Tanya's other trappings.
This is what stones and sticks transmit
when we are quiet. Chairs and tables, dishes and cups.
The minutiae of Judaic law perhaps only
a pretext to raise sparks of light
back to original form, the originally unformed.
To make a seder out of all this stuff that is not stuff.

**Beautiful Gardens**

These are the beautiful gardens where children grow
   psychiatric disorders.
There is a smaller house, much like a turtle, where
   someone lives.
He might be the curator of despondent plants called
   children, usually he is.
We will think only with our bodies, you say; we will
   dedicate this week
to being only a body; we will go to the hamburger place.
Landscape artists and curators of gardens will say that
   thirty days
have passed while waiting. I don't think that they are
   lying, though maybe
to the landscape and the gardens. Among other
   pretensions
is the pretension that I was waiting for anything but
   your promise
of passing our days walking to the hamburger place, of
   waking together hungry.

## Yester Night

Yester night I dreamt a long bright sword
Surrendered to King Richard, whose return
Is herald to a Lionhearted Age,
From our dimension hidden, beyond scale
And scope of time's constraint upon our life.
Here dream is not mere dream and all grows young;
Arrival and departure are the same.
I recognized the red hair of that King
As though encoded in another brain,
Wherein the memory of events long past
Become the moving picture meant to be.
That fleeting frame is precious to the mind
That cannot capture or replay the scene
Like water lost into eternal stream.

**Echad**

You are my future; I am your past.
Everything told, I tell myself.
Let our conversation outlast
Temporal vessels, casting words
Into so many echoing worlds.

**Compass**

My single compass is the midnight sun,
A star above the mortal world,
From which all poems have begun,
The sound of light that goes unheard
Until the one who listens is no more
And only song remains throughout the whole
Expanse of space, forever and before
You think of how to reach a timeless goal.
I am what that sound has always been,
A darkness that is bright beyond compare,
A vajra lamp that does not shine for him
In whom the dark and light are not a pair.
As this world dies, the midnight sun outshines
What never was, the truth and every lie.

**Naropa**

Naropa fought the great pandits of his day
in dialectic debate, before a divine hag
showed up, ugly and mad, literate only
in the language of that skylike reality
beyond philosophy. When she questioned
all this chattering intellect, he finally entered
stupefaction, a state without hope, without home.
Yet I'm still wedded to a wellspring of words,
tethered to tomes of learning,
and might only know renunciation
when my breath rattles without elocution,
my hands shake, incapable of mudra then.

## Minerva Again

If the Owl of Minerva flies at dusk
this a dilapidated owl. If the Dawn Horse
runs the primordial plain, this is a staggering pony.
Arrows as common as summer rains,
the confused calm before, during, and after the storm.
"Worship me with swords" now a theosophical
platitude, from black magic's major arcana.
Be careful what one's wit is for, wherefore one wishes
to turn the seeming sequence of time and space
into order reversed, moving in dumb diagonals.

**First Thing**

Fate was the first thing that happened, after all.
Cause and effect ambulate together
around the austere tree of life, and are the same.
Prior to all happenings, is where another
joy, extensionless, abounds.
I can't see what my eyes do not indicate,
nor can indication truly denote my eyes.
A dog barks in the distance, in the morning
birds will chirp. The distance is barking
dogs, the birds the morning chirping.
Maybe the body is always asleep,
night or day, but doesn't know it.
What we call dreaming is wakefulness too,
what we call waking, only more
garrulous sleep, wherein real voices speak.

## Christmas

How fanciful I was, when fecund winter
Brought fortune one Christmas —
We talked of apocryphal gospels
Around your mother's table, and a cloud
Of unknowing fell upon me, upon your home,
All was a resurrection of mystery
Before I was you and you were me
And we were as a synchronicity entwined.
Love without form is Christ the true vine,
Yet still everywhere such rapture
Means less without our embodied time,
How much less as the heart
Of a cold epoch approaches
And joyous nights fall out of focus?

**Shekhinah**

Old age began soon after our love-craze.
Beside the single word that is your gaze
All is a palace denoting empty phrases,
Entire canons of verse entombing me,
Orchards of decay and infertility.
O that I could see you in the Sabbath Queen,
Her incorporeal body's perfect gleam.
Hard to imagine what the eyes don't see:
Light no longer penetrates the lids,
As if irises were black holes sucking in
Some vestiges of sun or moonlit glow.
I cannot say wherefore all things must go
But know that vapor rises into sky,
Falls down again on earth that once was dry.

**Chen**

I know myself less these days,
& by extension you me, I think, though maybe not.
I wonder, do you forgive
my decathection, after so many years?
You're a poet now, you were a poet then.
I have been a kind of brainstorm,
I didn't intend it so. I suppose there is only one
forgiveness, as there is only one
moment, forever asking we attend it.
There must be a timeless place, prior to words,
where this forgiveness is possible.
Psychosis can get you there
but I wouldn't recommend it.
There must be a time where words
are taking place, & claim priority
over what is possible:
I wish I were my self before the storm.
The one who loved the english language
so much I had to befriend you.

**Bipolarity**

In my system, sated, made of chemicals,
Wellbutrin and more precious Lexapro,
Without which in some bed catatonic lay: I
Would not move, in erstwhile times delay
All things to other calendars and realms,
Procrastinate the daylight to the fell
Of dark and doomed decay, muted
Like an afterlife in lull; not forgetting
Aripiprazole, lest moods take too much flight,
Falling to depression's deepest floor;
I ingest what nature from me hath deprived
So that these words delight and come alive.
I bless what creature in me hath survived,
So that its world alights and even thrives.

## Alphabetical Contents

| | | | |
|---|---|---|---|
| Banzai | 17 | Merlin | 36 |
| Beautiful Gardens | 42 | Minerva Again | 47 |
| Beginning | 34 | Nachman's Chair | 9 |
| Béla, Planting | 27 | Naropa | 46 |
| Bipolarity | 52 | No Taste | 15 |
| Breakfast | 20 | Olam | 1 |
| Chen | 51 | Planets Turn | 2 |
| Christmas | 49 | Polemos | 14 |
| Compass | 45 | Queen of Swords | 3 |
| Echad | 44 | Reception | 38 |
| Evening | 31 | Seder | 41 |
| Even Mount Sumeru | 33 | Shekhinah | 50 |
| Exodus | 18 | Sidney | 26 |
| First Morning | 23 | Station Grey | 29 |
| First Thing | 48 | Summer | 16 |
| Four Octobers | 21 | Talmud | 4 |
| Friend | 13 | The Headless... | 10 |
| Heretics | 11 | Vilna Gaon | 40 |
| If the Owl... | 12 | Waiting | 19 |
| July | 5 | Waves | 37 |
| Jus Soli | 24 | Winter Cosmogony | 8 |
| Kyle | 28 | Yaakov | 6 |
| Landscape Artist | 22 | Yester Night | 43 |
| Lexicon | 7 | Young Alaina | 30 |
| Marlowe | 39 | Zoe | 32 |
| Mercutio | 35 | | |

**About the Author**

Zachary Horvitz was born in Paris and attended primary school at Ecole Active Bilingue Jeannine Manuel. Inauspiciously, his teacher crumpled up his first poem and tossed it into the trash can. Mr. Horvitz occasionally attended classes at Reed College in Portland, Oregon, and Bennington College, in Bennington, Vermont, where he majored in intramural soccer. He lives in Newton, Massachusetts, and can often be found in contemplation at L'Aroma Cafe & Bakery or exploring the stacks at the Newton Free Library.

*Special thanks to Avery Bargar.*

www.ingramcontent.com/pod-product-compliance
Lightning Source LLC
Chambersburg PA
CBHW020301010526
44108CB00037B/511